Mimicry
and camouflage

JILL BAILEY

D1301386

Facts On File Publications
New York, New York ● Oxford, England

Library of Congress Catalog Card Number:

87-33149

Designed and produced by BLA Publishing Limited,
East Grinstead, Sussex, England.

A member of the **Ling Kee Group**
LONDON·HONG KONG·TAIPEI·SINGAPORE·NEW YORK

Phototypeset in Britain by BLA Publishing/Composing Operations
Colour origination by Planway Ltd
Printed and bound in Italy by New Interlitho

10 9 8 7 6 5 4 3 2 1

Note to the reader
On page 59 of this book you will find the glossary. This gives brief explanations of
words which may be new to you.

Contents

The world of disguise

You are about to enter a secret world, a world full of hidden creatures, of animals so cleverly disguised that their enemies walk right over them without seeing them. It is a world of deceit, where living creatures may look like stones, plants may look like animals, and animals may look like plants.

In the world of disguise, surprise also plays a part. An apparently harmless caterpillar may suddenly rise up and hiss fiercely, showing huge eyes in a snake-like face. Or a dull brown moth may roll on its side to show a striped wasp-like body, curled up ready to sting.

Hunters and hunted

All these disguises are part of the fight for survival. Animals whose disguises help them to avoid being discovered by their enemies will live longer and produce more offspring. But the hunters can profit from disguise, too. If you can look like a dead leaf, your prey may well come within arm's reach.

Praying mantids that look like flowers capture flies that actually land on them to search for nectar. Even large hunters like lions benefit from coats that match the brown of the dry grassland in which they stalk their zebra and antelope prey.

▲ There are two moths on this tree trunk. Can you spot them?

Camouflage tactics

A lot of animals have colors that closely match the usual surroundings in which they live. Grasshoppers have green and brown striped bodies to match the pattern of grass blades and shadows; fish are silvery blue like the sea; and birds match the leafy branches so well that we cannot usually see them even when their song tells us that they are close at hand.

Many insects and other small animals come out to feed at night, when many of their enemies are asleep. Some insects spend the whole day resting out in the open, relying on their camouflage to avoid being discovered.

▲ A female paraque or white-necked nightjar sits perfectly still on her eggs, her eyes almost closed so as not to give away her presence. She cannot afford to be seen. If she has to fly away to escape a predator, the eggs will get chilled, and they will not hatch.

Nature's mimics

Some animals are shaped like objects in their surroundings. There are praying mantids that look like stones, grasshoppers that look like sticks, caterpillars that look like bird droppings, and even fish that look like seaweed. Some quite harmless animals look like much more dangerous animals, so their enemies avoid them. "Mimicry" is the name given to these disguises, in which the animal looks like something else.

We do it too

Humans use camouflage, too. Soldiers wear clothes that are covered in patches of brown, green, and yellow. This makes them very difficult to see at a distance when they are out in the open countryside. Bird-watchers often wear similar clothes for the same reason. They also build hides — tents made in camouflage colors or covered in branches so that the birds will think they are bushes and not fly away.

We use mimicry, too. Everyone knows what fun it is to go to a masquerade party. How often do you put on special clothes to make yourself look older?

▼ Sea anemones, sea slugs, prawns, crabs, and fish all look like pieces of sargassum weed. Among the sargassum fronds, hunter and hunted live side by side, often without recognizing each other. How many animals can you spot in this picture?

The secret world of the sargassum weed

Far out in the middle of the Atlantic Ocean is a vast sea of sargassum weed, a kind of golden brown seaweed that floats in clumps on the surface of the ocean. It is a strange little world, in which everything is camouflaged.

More about ⟫ Praying mantids p 40 Snake-like caterpillars p 49
Bird-dropping mimics p 39 ⟫

The art of camouflage

▲ The deadly stonefish is covered in knobbly lumps that look like pieces of rock or coral. When a smaller fish comes within reach, it opens its huge mouth and sucks it in.

Have you ever visited a wild place such as a nature reserve and been rather disappointed not to see the animals you were expecting to see? Well, they probably *are* there — its just that you don't see them because they look so much like their surroundings. We say they are "camouflaged."

This book is all about camouflage and other ways in which animals deceive people (and other animals) who are looking for them. Perhaps when you have read it, you will be able to see more of the wild animals around you.

See-through disguise

Under water, a transparent body often makes a good disguise. The background shows through, so the animal appears to be part of it.

▼ The common shrimp is transparent by night (*top*) and camouflaged by day.

This shrimp is transparent at night, when the fading light from the sky above shines right through it as it swims in search of food. By day it becomes colored to match the sand in which it hides.

Secrets of success

Camouflaged animals not only match their natural surroundings in color, they also have matching patterns of colors. Sometimes animals will hide their shadows with special color patterns or even fringes. Sometimes they add shadow-like patterns for

disguise. Woodland butterflies often have yellow spots on their wings that look like patches of sunlight on dead leaves. By clever use of mock shadow patterns, frogs can look like flattened leaves, and moths can look like fat twigs.

Other animals disguise their outlines by having wavy edges, or by tucking their legs underneath them or by flattening themselves against tree trunks. Animals that mimic seaweed or lichens often have knobbly surfaces to match.

Choosing your background

Some animals, such as the chameleons and many frogs, toads, and fish can change their color to match their background. Others choose their background to match their color. Flower-mimic moths, which are always found on matching flowers, seek out the correct flowers by their smell.

Sea hares are slug-like animals that live in the sea near coasts. They feed on red seaweeds when they are very young, gradually moving on to brown and purple seaweeds as they get older. Their color changes to match the sea-weeds they are feeding on. But if they are kept on only one color of seaweed, they still change color as they grow older. If given a choice, they will seek out matching-colored seaweeds to feed on.

Seeing straight

Not all animals can see in color, so we have to be careful about assuming that animals appear as well camouflaged to them as they do to us.

On the other hand, some animals that appear to be very bright to us would be less obvious to them. When you see only in black and white, the pattern of light and shade is very important, so the camouflage pattern may be more important than its color.

Feeding on color

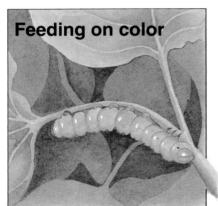

Where food is brightly colored, the animals may take in the color chemicals with their food and use them to color their own bodies. In this way, the animals come to match their background. Some sea slugs feed on algae, small seaweed-like plants, and absorb their pigments. The white and yellow colors of some butterflies and the green colors of caterpillars come from their food.

▼ A camouflaged sea slug grazes on the algae that give it its purple coloring.

More about 〉〉 Transparent animals p 29 Leaf-like frogs p 24 Twig-mimic moths p 25
Changing color p 10, 11, 16-19 Disguising outlines p 22, 23 〉

Changing with the seasons

In the cooler parts of the world, the various colors of the landscape change with the seasons. In summer the land is green and brown, but in the winter it is white, covered in a blanket of snow and ice. An animal whose color matches the summer landscape will be very conspicuous as it crosses the snow in winter.

Nearer the equator, where there are distinct wet and dry seasons, insects that match the green vegetation of the wet season are no longer well camouflaged when the dry season arrives and the grasses and flowers wither to a dull brown. So, animals that need to remain camouflaged during both these seasons, have to change their coats.

Warm winter coats

Some birds and mammals that live in cold climates change their coats in the autumn as the landscape changes color. Gradually the old hairs or feathers are shed, and new white ones grow through in their place. This is called molting. Their coats change a little at a time — you don't see bald mammals running around, or featherless birds unable to fly! Winter fur is often thicker than summer fur, providing extra warmth as well as camouflage. Winter feathers may also be fluffier. In spring, another molt takes place, and the animals grow their summer coats.

Winter gray

Even mammals of warmer climates, which do not always have a layer of snow in winter, often change color from reddish brown to grayish brown in winter. This helps them to blend in better with the bare trees of woodlands and hedgerows.

▶ Snowshoe hare in summer (*above*) and winter (*below*).

Telltale signs of winter

How do animals "know" when to change coats? If they wait until the chill winter frosts and snow arrive, it will be too late to start growing the new coat. Weather signals are unreliable. Most animals can detect the decreasing length of day, and this will trigger the change in their coats. Whatever the weather, the days get shorter in autumn and longer in spring, so providing the animals with a reliable "clock."

Other signals may also be used. Stoats become white in winter in the Arctic. This white fur is called ermine.

But in Scotland, where some winters are much colder than others, stoats become white in cold winters, but not in milder ones.

Matching the grass

Many insects are able to respond to the changing backgrounds by producing different colored larvae or pupae. Caterpillars of the owl butterfly are green in spring, when the plants on which they feed are green. But, when they molt their skins later in the summer, the new skins are brown so that the caterpillars match the drying plants and vegetation.

▼ Owl butterfly caterpillars in early summer.

▼ Owl butterfly caterpillars in late summer.

The chivalrous ptarmigan

The male ptarmigan does not put on his spring plumage as soon as the female. In the spring he is still wearing a mixture of white feathers and patches of mottled brown when the female is already brown all over. She is very well camouflaged on the moorland newly exposed by the melting snow. The male is more likely to attract the attentions of predators than the female, perhaps making it less likely that a predator will discover the female sitting on her precious eggs.

Swallowtail and cabbage-white butterflies produce greenish pupae (chrysalids) in early summer, but brown ones later in the year.

Sometimes they produce a mixture of the two. This makes sure that some escape detection by predators if unusual weather causes the grass to stay green longer or turn brown sooner.

More about ≫ Animals that look like plants p 40, 41
Fur and feathers p 13, 19

What is color?

When you look at an object, what you are really seeing is light that has been reflected by the object you are looking at. Light enters your eye and causes changes in certain chemicals. Messages are sent by the nerves to the brain to tell it of these changes, and your brain will then interpret this information as sight.

Multicolored light

Light is made up of several waves of energy. Some of the waves have more energy than others. Each wave produces a different color of light. Light waves usually travel in straight lines. This is why you cannot see what is around a corner.

When light waves hit a solid surface, their energy may be absorbed by the solid substance, or the light waves may be reflected — they bounce off the surface. We see only those light waves that are reflected. Some surfaces reflect only certain colors of light. For example, green grass blades reflect green light and absorb the other colors. A black dress absorbs all the colors of light, while a white one reflects them all.

Bending the light

Some substances, such as glass and water, are see-through or transparent. Light can pass through them. But when light waves pass from the air to another substance, such as water, they are bent — we say they are refracted. Some colors of light are bent more than others. This is what happens when white light is passed through a glass prism. As the different color light waves bend, they separate, so you can see all the seven colors that go to make up the white light. This band of different colors is called the light spectrum.

▶ White light passing through a prism splits into different colors.

The puzzle of the bright red prawn

In the depths of the oceans, many prawns are bright red. You might expect that they would all be gobbled up by hungry fish. But, in fact, the prawns are camouflaged. Because light rays are refracted in water, only blue light reaches the ocean depths. There is no red light. These creatures appear red only because they reflect the red light supplied by the photographer's lamp. Without the lamp, they would appear quite black — almost invisible in the dark ocean deeps.

All washed out

The blue-fronted Amazon parrot has green feathers that turn dull brown in the rain. As the feathers become wet, they lose their ability to reflect and refract light, so the green color is lost.

Shimmering colors

Fur, feathers, scales, and the hard shells of insects all reflect light. Their slightly dissimilar surfaces reflect different colors of light to produce patterned coats. Sometimes the surfaces also have many tiny grooves and ridges on them, which are far too small to see. These reflect the light in special patterns. Or there may be several fairly transparent layers, which bend the light of each color at a different angle, and so produce various refraction patterns.

These structures can create many different color effects. They range from the shiny metallic blues and greens of hummingbirds, kingfishers, and peacocks, to the iridescent shimmering colors of mother of pearl, butterfly wings, and beetles. These appear to change color as the animals move, and you see them from different angles.

▲ A close-up view of the wing of a Madagascan Croesus moth.

Combination colors

Many animal colors are due to a combination of pigments and the surface structure of their bodies. Light reflected from the surface of scales or feathers blends with light reflected from the pigments below to produce new colors.

The colorful patterns of many lizards, fish, squid, and octopuses are due to several layers of pigment cells. Each layer of cells contains different colored pigments, which expand by varying amounts in different places.

Colour from air and oil

Fur and feathers are often gray because they contain trapped air bubbles, which reflect all the colors of light. The gold and yellow colors of many cockerels and the bright red caps of woodpeckers are formed by light reflected off oils and fats. Crystals of guanine, a waste material produced by animals, create the bright mirror-like effect of many fish scales.

◄ Rudd and bleak have silvery "mirror" sides.

More about ⟩⟩ Deep-sea animals p 28, 29 Pigment cells p 14, 16-19
Color in animals p 14, 15, 57

A patchwork of colors

▲ A close look at the fin of a stickleback shows the star-like pigment cells containing the black pigment melanin.

▼ The squid has several layers of pigment cells, each containing a different colored pigment.

The colors of many plants and animals are due to the presence of pigments. These chemicals are produced by the body, and reflect particular colors. Pigments are found in special cells, which look like wiggly stars. These pigments are able to move in the cells. Sometimes they are spread through the arm of the stars, and sometimes they are just concentrated in the center of the cell. Because of this, some animals are able to change their color, as the different colored pigments spread out or contract.

Pretty pigments

Pigment cells are usually found just below the surface of the skin. In most mammals and birds, the colors of their skins are hidden by fur or feathers, but in animals with very little hair, like whales, elephants, hippos, and rhinos, the color of the skin pigments is easy to see.

Pigments have other uses besides camouflage. Brown and black pigments protect the skin from the harmful parts of the sun's rays. Dark pigments also absorb heat, while pale ones reflect it.

Pigments are also found in the dead parts of the body — hairs, fur, feathers, scales, the shells of insects and crustaceans, and the scales covering the wings of moths and butterflies.

Borrowed colors

In the oceans and in moist places on land, there are millions of tiny microscopic plants, too small to see, called algae. Like flowering plants, algae make their own food using light energy, which they trap with special light-absorbing pigments.

In the oceans, some algae live inside the tissue of animals. Here they have protection from the world outside, yet they can still absorb light that passes through the host animal's transparent skin.

The brilliantly colored mantles of clams and many of the bright colors of corals are due to the colored pigments of these algae.

Living camouflage

The sloth, which lives in the tropical forests of Central and South America, hangs upside down among the branches. Its fur has a greenish tinge which closely matches its background. This is due to a slimy layer of green algae, which grow on the sloth's fur. In wet weather, the algae look green, but in dry weather they become brownish, so the sloth still matches the drying vegetation around it.

Circulating colors

Blood contains colorful pigments that are used to carry oxygen around the body. The blood pigment of humans and many other animals is red, while the blood of cuttlefish is usually pale blue or even colorless. Blood pigments only give an animal color where it has no covering of fur or feathers, or where its outer surface is transparent. The uakari monkey has a bright red face, which becomes even redder when it is angry as more blood is allowed close to the skin surface. The red color of chicken combs, and the red of many prawns, is due to their blood pigments.

Blood pigments also get broken down in the body to form other pigments, usually brown or yellow. These are the colorings that make the blotches and speckles used to camouflage birds' eggs, and also the browns and yellows of many animals.

King of the colors

The cockerel is a master of color. His bright red comb and wattle are due to red blood pigments showing through his transparent skin. The bright yellows and reds on his neck are due to light reflected off oils and fats. The dark colors on his body are produced by pigments, and the iridescent metallic colors of his tail are due to light being reflected from microscopic ridges in his tail feathers.

▼ A cock jungle fowl crowing.

Changing color

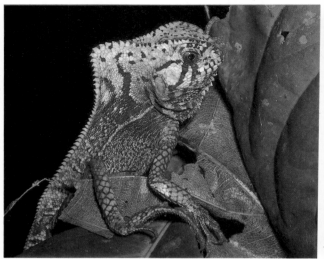

▲ The casque-head lizard from Costa Rica is a close relative of the chameleon, and is just as good at changing color.

Background colors don't always stay the same. Some leaves change color with the seasons, and dead leaves change color when they get damp. Colors alter as the light gets brighter in the morning and duller in the evening. An animal may need to move from one place to another to hunt or feed. It may need to leave the trees and travel over the brown woodland floor, or it may need to cross a patch of bright sunshine. It is rather difficult to imagine a camouflage that would work equally well for the animal in all of these very different situations.

Some animals get around this problem by adjusting their color to match the changing background. Many different animals can change color — lizards, octopuses, squid, toads, fish, prawns, crabs, and a host of small soft-bodied invertebrates. There are several ways of changing color, and many different signals can be used to trigger a color change in animals.

Master of the art

Chameleons have always fascinated people. When sitting on a leafy branch in the daylight, the chameleon will be green, with patches of black and pale brown that resemble the shadows of the bushes around it. As the evening approaches, and the light begins to fade, the color of the chameleon changes to grayish-green, then to pale fawn with yellow patches. In the dark the chameleon may become black all over. These changes in color take only about 15 minutes.

The chameleon does not only change its color to match its background. If it is angry, it will develop deep orange spots and dark red patches, colors that signal danger to most animals.

Choosing the colors

The chameleon does not know it is changing color — the change is completely automatic. Its eyes and parts of its skin detect the colors of its surroundings and send signals to the brain. The brain then sends messages along nerves to tell the pigment cells to make the necessary changes in color.

A touch of color

Some animals are sensitive to the feel of their natural surroundings. European tree frogs change from green to silver-gray when they move from a tree trunk covered in soft algae to a patch of bare bark. Many experiments have shown that they detect the different surface by touch.

How is it done?

Changing color in an animal is not a simple process. The chameleon's colors are contained in special pigment cells in the skin. The way these cells are arranged gives the chameleon its pattern. Near the base of its skin are cells containing black pigment. Then comes a layer of cells that reflect white. Next comes a blue-reflecting layer, and above it a layer of yellow pigment cells. The different combinations of yellow, blue, white, and black give the chameleon its range of colors. The colors change when the pigments spread out or shrink in the cells.

In many fish, the eyes are the most important color detectors. Flatfish, such as plaice and sole, can match very closely the pattern of the seabed where they rest. A plaice put on a chess board will even become checkered. If a plaice is put on a board with its head and eye on one color, and the rest of the body on a contrasting color, the whole body develops the color of the part of the board its eyes can see.

▼ Common toad in forest on dry day (*top*) and wet day (*bottom*).

Wet and dry colors

Country folk say that you can forecast the weather just by looking at the colors of frogs and toads. Many frogs and toads change color in wet weather, becoming darker. Since frogs and toads usually live on the ground, and dead twigs and leaves become dark when wet, this change makes sure that they remain well camouflaged. They also change color according to their background. You may think you have several toads in your garden when, in fact, you have only one, but it looks a different color at different times.

More about ⟩⟩ Changing color p 10, 11, 18, 19 Pigments p 14, 15, 18, 19
Reflecting light p 12, 13

Fast colors

Different animals change color at different speeds. The chameleon takes about 15 minutes to change color, while young crabs take only 30 seconds. Sticklebacks change color in about four minutes, and groupers — large fish that live near coral reefs — can produce up to eight different patterns in just a few seconds.

Squid and octopuses can also change their color very rapidly. Sometimes it appears as if waves of color are pulsating across their bodies. Lots of different things set off these changes — anger, the sight of food, fear, and the color of the background. A squid that is changing color is a really amazing sight. Rosy flushes pulse across its body, and tiny flashing dots of red and gold come and go, and its pattern can change from tiny dots to bold stripes and eye-like patches. Scientists think squid may use color patterns to communicate with each other.

Nervous colors

These very rapid color changes take place in response to nerve signals. The pigments in the cells are attached to muscle fibers, and signals from the animal's brain, sent along the nerves, cause these muscle fibers to change the size and shape of pigments. This change happens very quickly. The color changes of the chameleon are caused by chemical messages sent by the brain, and are much slower. The octopus and squid use both nerve and chemical signals.

Courtship colors

Not all colors are used for camouflage. Some male birds, like the pheasant and peacock, grow brightly colored plumage in spring to attract mates. Female birds stay in camouflage colors, which protect them while they sit on their eggs. Fish like the stickleback also develop special bright breeding colors. Some male lizards blush bright red or puff out colorful throat sacs when they are angry — and when they are excited by the approach of a female.

▼ A dumpling squid from Australia.

▼ These baby squid show how small changes in the size of pigment patches can create a different pattern.

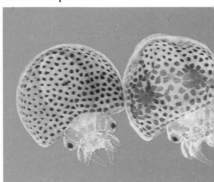

Living in the dark

Animals that live in dark caves, where there is usually no light to see by, are often pale pink — only their blood gives them color. However, many of these cave animals will gradually develop a dark color if they are brought into the light. Light is needed to trigger the development of the pigment cells.

The blushing octopus

The octopus is very difficult to spot when it is resting on the seabed, so closely do its colors match the rocks and sand around it. But, if the octopus is excited or annoyed, it shows a remarkable display of color. If you disturb it, it will turn deep crimson, wave its tentacles, and raise its body up and down. The sight of food — or of a female — will also make it blush.

▲ A starling in smart spring plumage. The smart white speckles at the tips of its feathers will wear off during the summer.

▼ The sight of an attractive female is enough to make an octopus blush.

Colors that wear out

Some colors don't last forever. The colors of bird feathers, reptile scales, and mammal fur become dull with age. They cannot change color quickly, because their pigments are fixed in dead cells. Snakes and lizards shed their skins from time to time as they grow. The colors of the new skin are much brighter and clearer than those of the old skin. Bird feathers wear down, and have to be renewed twice a year. Starlings have pretty speckled coats in spring and summer, but the white feather tips gradually wear away, and the starling loses its spots and looks duller.

More about ⟫ Changing color p 16, 17 Squid p 16 Feathers p 10-13

Hiding shadows

We learn to recognize objects by their shape as well as their color. Cows in a field stand out because they have a distinctive shape. Even in a black-and-white picture, they are easy to spot. But what generally makes shapes most conspicuous is their shadows. When you first draw a picture of an animal, it looks flat rather than solid until you put some shading on it. As you start to shade it, it begins to look more like a solid rounded object.

Animals are less easy to see on cloudy days, or in dim light, because their shadows are not so obvious. So, by disguising their shadows, they can blend in better with their background.

Shadows and shapes

Imagine a horse standing in a field in the sun. Where does its shadow fall? Part of it falls on the ground, and part on the horse. Its belly is in shade, and the sides of its head, neck, belly, and legs nearest the sun appear to be lighter than the other side. All these shadows help you to recognize the shape of the horse.

Camouflage shading

Many animals use color to disguise their shadows. They have pale bellies and darker backs — the reverse of the shadow effect. When their bellies are in shade, they match their backs. This type of coloring is called "counter-shading" — it counteracts the effects of shadows. Four-footed mammals usually have pale bellies and dark backs, and so do most birds.

Fish have bluish backs and pale bellies. When seen from the side, this disguises their shadows. When seen from below, their white bellies blend with the light coming from above. When seen from above, perhaps by a sea bird, their blue backs blend with the color of the ocean.

The bellies of flatfish are also pale, but if a flatfish is placed in a tank lit from below, its belly becomes dark, too. Seagulls and terns have pale bellies, so they are not easily seen by their fish prey. But when viewed from above, their blue-gray backs match the ocean below.

Upside down colors

Animals that live upside down, like the caterpillars that usually crawl along the undersides of leaves and twigs, have the opposite shading — their backs are pale and their bellies darker. Sea creatures that live and feed at the surface of the ocean also have this "reverse countershading," as do water insects like water boatmen and backswimmers.

◀ The impala has a dark back and pale belly to help conceal its shadow.

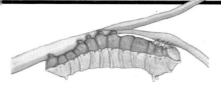

▲ The squeaking silkmoth caterpillar has a dark belly and a pale back because it spends its life upside down.

Frills and fringes

Most moths have fringes of hairs around the edges of their wings, which help to break up their outline. Flatfish have wavy fins running along their bodies, which dip down and touch the seabed and cast no shadow. Some lizards use flaps of skin to hide the shadow of their fat bellies and tails.

▲ The peacock flounder presses its fins into the sand to hide its shadow. Only around its mouth is a shadow cast on the seabed.

▶ These black skimmer chicks are flattening their bodies against the sand to hide their shadows.

Lying low

Animals can avoid casting shadows by lying low, and flattening their bodies against the ground. The young of birds that nest on the ground crouch down and stretch their necks out flat on the ground. Moths that rest on tree trunks during the day do not fold their wings tightly above their bodies. Instead, they press them flat against the tree trunk so that they do not cast a shadow. Tree frogs rest with their legs drawn in close to their bodies so that their bellies rest on the branch or leaf. Even in the sea, resting flatfish press their bodies close to the sand.

The nightjar, sitting on her eggs among the leaves on the woodland floor, shifts her position as the sun moves around the sky so that she is always facing it. In this position she does not cast much shadow.

The flying dragon

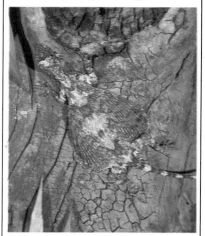

The Malaysian flying dragon has very large skin flaps stretching from its front legs to its back legs, which disguise its shadow. If the dragon wants to get from one tree to another, it leaps into the air and stretches out its legs. The skin flaps spread out like a parachute, and the lizard glides through the air to the next tree trunk.

More about ≫ Tricks with shadows p 24, 25 Disguising shapes p 22, 23, 26, 27
Caterpillars in disguise p 11, 30, 35, 37, 38, 39, 49

Changing shape

While shadows help us to detect the presence of animals, it is their shape that tells us what kind of animals they are. Movement of legs and head quickly give away their presence. The very presence of legs tells us that an object is an animal rather than a vegetable or a mineral, just as the presence of leaf shapes shows that it is a plant. There are several positions and patterns that help disguise the shape and outlines of animals.

► The mottled legs of this spider from Borneo are difficult to see.

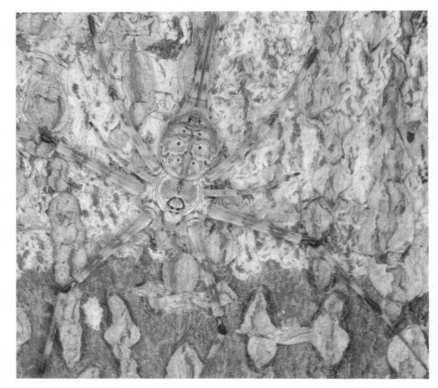

▼ This Australian stick insect is sitting face downward, with its legs pressed tight against the twig. Its wing cases stick out like a side twig.

Missing legs

The simplest kind of disguise is to tuck the legs in close to the body, which gives a smooth body outline instead of a leggy one. Frogs, toads, and grasshoppers do this when resting out in the open. Sometimes the effect can be improved by patterns of stripes and blotches that run continuously across both the body and legs when the legs are tucked in.

Some spiders and stick insects use the opposite tactic. They stretch their legs out in front and behind their long thin bodies so that the body and legs form a single stick-like shape. Antennae (feelers) also spoil the effect. They may be laid back along the body for disguise.

Spiders that rest with their legs spread out often have mottled legs that blend with the pattern of tree bark. Such horizontal stripes avoid the lines of solid color that signal legs. Many prawns have similar mottled patterns on their legs and antennae. Even bright red-and-white striped legs can be unrecognizable against the mixture of background colors that are found on a coral reef.

Blurring the edges

Animals usually have smooth outlines. Many butterflies have checkered borders to their wings, so their outlines are less easily recognized. Fringes on the wings also produce a blurred indistinct outline, and transparent wavy fins can have a similar blurring effect in fish.

Stonefish, scorpionfish, and anglerfish, which look just like stones, have knobbly surfaces, and are often covered in what look like tiny pieces of seaweed but are actually flaps of skin. Their body surface looks like the knobbly rocks and corals around them. This camouflage is so good that other animals can step on them without noticing them — not a good idea, as stonefish have a row of poisonous spines along their backs.

This camouflage is mainly used to ambush their prey. These fish have enormous mouths. If a small fish passes close enough, the stonefish has only to open its mouth, and the inrush of water takes its dinner in with it.

A similar camouflage is used by insects that mimic lichens or mosses. Their bodies are covered with tiny plant-like scales which match their mossy background.

▲ Patterns that run continuously across the body and legs when at rest help to conceal the frog's legs.

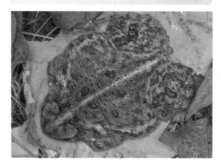

Thin as a shadow

The John Dory, or St. Peter's fish, is a very flat fish. When viewed from the front it looks just like a shadow or streak in the water. This helps it to ambush its prey. It has huge lips which can stretch out very fast to seize small water creatures passing by.

◄ With its legs drawn in, this toad does not look at all toad-like.

► The scorpionfish's head looks like a lump of seaweed.

More about ▷▷ Disguising shapes p 24-27 Ambushing prey p 29, 30, 40 Stonefish p 8
Frog and toad disguises p 17, 24, 47 Animals that look like plants p 40, 41

Tricks with shadows

The horned frog (above and left) lives among the dead leaves on the jungle floor. It is one of many leaf-mimic frogs.

Shadows can help us to recognize the shapes of plants and animals. But animals can also use false shadows to make them look as if they have a different shape. False shadows can make thick things look thin, and flat objects look well-rounded and fat.

Clever shading

Many insects like moths and grasshoppers mimic dead leaves. In the Far East and in South America, there are frogs and toads that live on the forest floor and look like dead leaves. How does such a fat animal as a toad manage to look like a flat leaf?

Let us look at a leaf-mimic frog in more detail. Its body and the top of its head are flattened so that they do not have any give-away natural shadows. The top of its body and head extend over its sides as a ledge, which continues over the frog's eyes and snout. This gives it a flat surface about the same size, shape, and color as a leaf — brown, yellow, or gray, with darker patches. Along the toad's shoulders, tiny raised ridges resemble the veins of an old, dead leaf. Immediately below the folds of skin, the body is a dark brown color, which looks like the shadow cast by the edge of a leaf. The real

shadow of the ledge of skin above adds to the effect. The toad's legs are also dark brown, to look like part of this shadow. The result is that the toad looks like an old leaf casting its shadow on the woodland floor.

Leaf-like grasshoppers and moths use similar coloring and shading to leaf-mimic toads. Often their wings have patterns that look like the branching veins of a leaf, and clever shading gives the impression that the leaf is starting to crumple between the veins. Some moths with perfectly flat wings look like bits of dead leaf with curled-up sides.

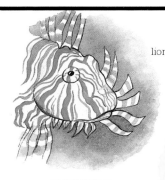

lionfish

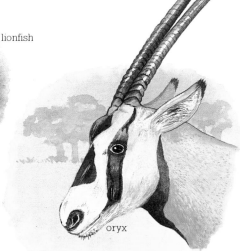

oryx

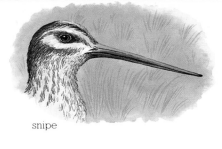

snipe

woodpecker

chameleon

Eye shadow

Eyes often give away an animal's presence, especially if the light catches them. Some camouflaged animals have dark stripes running across their heads that pass through the eyes, so that they do not show up as round blobs. This disguise is used by many fish. Fish have no eyelids, so patterns are the only way they can hide their eyes.

Birds such as waders, which nest on the ground, often have eyestripes. These birds are well camouflaged, but their eyes would give them away. Other birds, like the nightjar, simply close their eyes. Eyestripes allow the bird to keep watch and still stay camouflaged.

Some birds and fish use patches of color instead. There are so many colored patches on their heads that it is extremely difficult to see which are the eyes.

Making flat shapes fat

A few moths look just like broken twigs. Their heads and wing tips have a very sharply defined pale patch like the broken ends of a twig. These moths rest with their wings held together above their bodies to create the impression of a rounded twig. The correct shadow effect is produced because the folded wings are pale on top and darker below.

Mammals, birds, frogs, and toads have the advantage of eyelids that can be drawn over the eyes. Chameleons have eyes almost covered in scales that match their heads. Some snakes have ridges of scales above their eyes, so that the eyes cannot be seen from above, perhaps by a hungry bird.

▼ This prominent moth from Costa Rica is disguised as a broken twig.

More about ⟩⟩ Leaf mimics p 7, 31, 32, 35, 40, 41 Hiding eyes p 6, 26, 34
Disguising shapes p 20-23, 26-28

Optical illusions

It may seem surprising to learn that some of the most bright and colorful animals are actually camouflaged. Bold color patterns can help to disguise an animal's shape by dividing it into a number of blocks of color whose shape does not resemble anything in particular. This kind of coloring, which disguises an animal's outline by appearing to break up its shape, is called "disruptive coloration." It has produced some quite bizarre and strange-looking animals, with spectacular colors and patterns.

Mix and match

The pajama cardinal fish takes no chances. A dark stripe divides its shape in two, so there is no longer a clear fish outline to be seen. Its head matches the corals around it, and the round shape of its eye is disguised by two bright yellow stripes, which also help to disguise the shape of its head. Its rear half is spotted and, from a little distance away, the cardinal fish will not even appear to be a solid object. To complete the effect, the rear fins and tail are transparent.

▼ A pajama cardinal fish on a coral reef. Many of our most colorful animals are found on coral reefs, where blocks of color on their bodies are easily mistaken for patches of coral or algae.

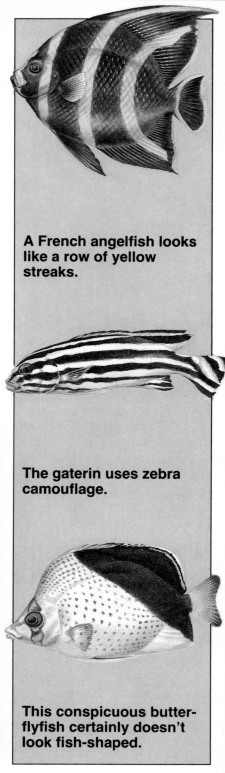

A French angelfish looks like a row of yellow streaks.

The gaterin uses zebra camouflage.

This conspicuous butter-flyfish certainly doesn't look fish-shaped.

Spots

With speckles and spots covering the skin, there are no bold lines of color boundaries, and no solid shapes that can be recognized. A speckled or spotted coat is almost invisible in the middle distance. In woods, the sunlight tends to stream through gaps in the branches like small spotlights on the woodland floor. Pale spots on a brown coat mimic the sunspots on brown leaves. Deer often use this kind of camouflage, and so do some woodland butterflies, whose wings are edged with yellow "eye" patterns. Very few birds are spotted, but many have mottled plumage, which produces a similar effect.

Spots are often used to camouflage the hunters as well as the hunted. Cheetahs, leopards, and many other large wild cats have very beautiful spotted coats. Sadly, this has led to thousands of them being hunted and killed for their skins.

▲ How many zebra can you count? Striped animals are particularly difficult to distinguish when there are large numbers of them together. Zebra live in big herds, and when they are on the move it is difficult for a predator to tell where one animal starts and another ends.

Stripes for survival

Stripes are a very effective way of breaking up the body outline. From a distance, they seem to merge into the background, and so no solid shape is visible. Stripes that run at right angles to the body shape form the most successful camouflage.

The zebra is striped all over. The stripes change from vertical to horizontal halfway along its back. This makes for more confusion. When viewed from behind, the horizontal stripes run at right angles to the zebra's shape to produce maximum effect. If the zebra needs to run away from predators, this is the view its enemies will get!

Zebras may not look very well camouflaged when seen in photographs, most of which are taken in broad daylight. But they are at greatest risk at dusk, when hungry lions are in search of supper. In this dim light, their camouflage is extremely effective.

◀ From a distance, cheetahs are difficult to spot.

More about 〉〉 Disguising shapes p 22-25 Spots and stripes p 25, 34, 44, 45, 52
Butterfly camouflage p 34, 40, 41 Fish disguises p 8, 23, 28, 32, 34, 41

Lights in the deep

▲ The lanternfish, at the top of the picture, has rows of light organs on its belly to disguise its shadow. The hatchetfish has mirror sides for camouflage. It is so flat and thin that if seen from the front it looks like a streak or a shadow in the water.

The open ocean is a place of shimmering clear water, with ever moving patterns of sunlight and wind-ruffled water. The surface waters are brilliantly lit, but as you go deeper the light changes. The scene becomes deeper and deeper blue, until at last there is only a faint hint of light from above and complete darkness below. Except for the occasional patches of floating seaweed, there is no really solid background, and no constant colors to match. So, most deep-sea animals have their own special kinds of disguises.

Lighting up

Deeper in the ocean, dark shadows are still a problem. Many deep-sea fish have upward-looking eyes to detect prey that is passing overhead. These are clearly silhouetted against the light above. Here, there is so little light that colors cannot be seen. Instead, deep-sea fish often have special structures that produce light. Rows of tiny luminous dots line their bellies, helping to disguise their shadows. A predator swimming below these fish will be looking at these rows of lights against the brighter water above.

Many deep-sea animals produce light. Octopuses, prawns, shrimps, and squid all have light organs rather like those of the fish. Even animals that live on the dark ocean floor, such as starfish, sea cucumbers, sea spiders, corals, and worms, produce light, but nobody is sure why they do it.

Mirrors in the deep

Another disguise is to have very shiny mirror-like sides. These reflect whatever light there is, instead of looking like a solid shape. Since the scenery down there is dark, the mirrors will look dark, too. In the deepest of the ocean deeps, three or four miles (five or six kilometers) down, there is no light, and most fish are simply black. Hunting here is done by smell or touch, or simply by having a very large mouth and swimming along with it wide open, hoping that something will fall in!

Luminous lures

Even in near darkness, some deception is possible. The deep-sea anglerfish has a luminous lure on its chin, a long worm-like structure that it waggles to look like a worm or small fish. This attracts inquisitive fish. As the fish come within reach, the angler suddenly opens its huge mouth, sucking them in.

Some tiny shrimp-like animals use light to make themselves look much bigger. When the light organs on their antennae and at the tips of their abdomens light up, they look three times bigger than they are.

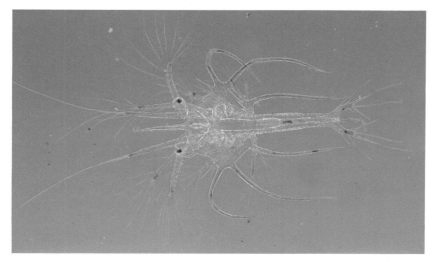

▲ The transparent larva of a prawn.

▼ As well as a luminous lure, the viperfish has light organs inside its mouth to lure its prey still closer.

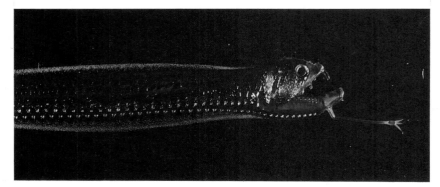

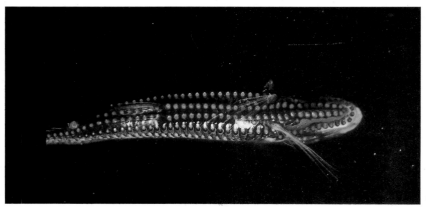

▲ Light organs on the belly of a deep-sea fish.

Safety at the surface

The animals that live near the surface of the water face danger from above and from below. Seabirds hunt them from the sky, and fish feed on them from below. Seen from below, anything with a solid outline will easily show up as a shadow against the bright light.

Small animals overcome this by being transparent. Their shapes are difficult to see against the bright sky, and the birds above see only the blue of the ocean showing through their bodies. There are millions of tiny transparent animals in the oceans, most of them too small to see. The young of prawns, crabs, sea snails, starfish, and fish all have see-through bodies.

Larger surface-dwelling animals rely on counter-shading. So, they are colored blue on the top and are white underneath.

More about 〉〉 Lures p 33 Transparent animals p 8, 45
Countershading p 20, 21

Keeping still

An important part of many disguises is the need to keep still. However well an animal matches its background, movements are likely to attract unwanted attention.

Moths, caterpillars, and tree frogs, which come out at night but rest out in the open by day, usually blend in very well with the bark or leaves on which they sit. However, they have to remain quite still all day.

The living dead

Some animals mimic objects that cannot move, such as twigs, stones, lichens, or fallen dead leaves. One such twig mimic is the European prominent moth. If prodded, it will fall over without moving its wings, just like a twig.

The stick caterpillar can stay "frozen" in its twig-like position all day. A slender girdle of silk anchors it to the twig, and this helps it to remain sticking out at a steep angle. This position makes the caterpillar look like the side branch of a twig.

Deadly still

Some predators use their camouflage to help them ambush their prey. The chameleon remains almost motionless, gripping its branch with special clinging feet that curve all the way around the twig. Its long tail can also be curled around a branch to help it balance. If it needs to stalk its prey, it creeps forward extremely slowly, one foot at a time.

▲ It is difficult to believe that this stick-like caterpillar will become a beautiful moth.

Mantids that look like green leaves, dead leaves, or flowers stay quite still, waiting for their prey to come to them. The vine snake of Central America is extremely thin, with a very long body. Its brownish mottled color closely resembles the stem of a vine. The snake hangs down from a branch, motionless and twisted like a vine, and waits to ambush passing birds.

Under the sea, the deadly stonefish lies quite still on the seabed. It looks so much like a stone or a piece of coral that its unwary prey will often climb over it without even recognizing it.

▼ A vine snake lies in wait for passing birds. It can hold a third of its long body rigid in space, waving it gently to and fro like a vine in the breeze.

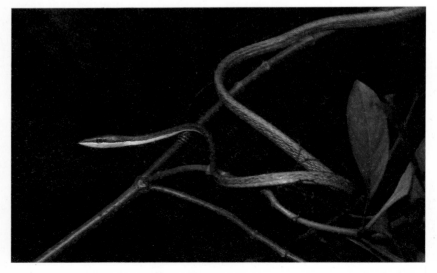

Playing possum

When they are attacked, some animals pretend to be dead. Many predators will not eat dead animals. Praying mantids and cats must kill their prey before they will eat it. Other predators may be attracted only by the movement of their prey, and they appear to overlook the animal as soon as it stops moving.

That often-used phrase "playing possum" comes from the American possum, which pretends to be dead when attacked. Many other kinds of animals do this. Beetles will drop to the ground and lie on their backs. Spiders roll over and curl up their legs, looking like a cast-off spider skin. Mantids and stick insects "freeze" if they are threatened by predators. Some snakes roll over on their back and let their head fall back to complete the effect.

Bird branch

The potoo rests by day. It stands completely still, with its head pointing upward and its eyes shut tight, so that it looks just like a broken tree stump or branch. It always chooses the tip of a stump to sit, where its camouflage will be most effective.

► The potoo points its head skyward and remains quite motionless, looking like the end of a tree stump.

▲ An American hog snake pretends to be dead.

Speed for safety

Keeping still is not always the best tactic in camouflage. Leaf-like mantids rock gently to and fro so that they look like dead leaves swaying in the breeze. Certain tropical spiders vibrate their webs so fast that you cannot see the spider sitting in the middle. The web becomes an almost invisible blur.

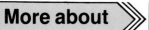

More about ≫

Twig mimics p 22, 25, 38 Leaf mimics p 11, 24, 32, 41, 49
Stone mimics p 8, 37-39

Acting the part

Some disguises just won't work! It's no good a fast-moving animal looking like a stick, as sticks don't move. The clown in the circus not only wears funny clothes and special makeup, he also acts the part. Many animal mimics have special behavior that makes their disguise even more effective.

A mean trick

Fish often suffer from nasty parasites that get in between their scales and bite them. Fish have no legs, so they cannot scratch themselves. But a little fish called the cleaner fish feeds on other fish's parasites, picking them off with its teeth. It advertises itself with a brightly striped body and a special zigzag dance. Big fish — large enough to eat the cleaner fish — often line up to be cleaned. They even open their mouths for the cleaner fish to clean their teeth.

The sabre-toothed blenny mimics the cleaner fish. It, too, is striped blue and black. It dances in front of big fish, but when they come to be cleaned, it darts in and bites a chunk of flesh off.

▶ Thorn-mimic bugs always sit so that the points of their thorns point downwards, like real thorns.

▲ An African leaf-fish rests on the seabed.

Drifting leaves

Several different fish look like floating dead leaves. The Amazon leaf-fish drifts head down near the surface of the water so that it can ambush passing fish. If it needs to swim, it uses its transparent fins. The Caribbean leaf-fish can also change its color to match any leaves that are floating nearby. If disturbed, it sinks in a zigzag path to the seabed, then darts away.

Ants that aren't

Ants bite, they squirt acid at intruders, and if you try to attack one, you soon find yourself attacking a whole army of them. Predators tend to avoid small animals that look like ants. There are ant-mimic bugs, mantids, spiders, and grasshoppers. These mimics improve their disguise by acting like ants, busily running to and fro, and waving their front legs like antennae.

Not all ant mimics are trying to avoid being attacked. Some deceive the ants themselves in order to get into their nests and eat their young. Ant-mimic jumping spiders mingle with the ants before pouncing on them.

The case of the vanishing frog

In South America, the Darwin's frog looks like an ordinary green frog. But, if it is threatened, it leaps into the nearest river, and rolls over on its back. It then just floats away, leaving its enemies wondering what happened. Its belly is the color of a dead leaf, and it draws in its legs and keeps quite still as it drifts along.

Beware of the worm

The snapping turtle lives in the warmer parts of the United States. It hunts its prey by sitting on the riverbed and opening its mouth wide. Inside its mouth is a pink fleshy lump that looks rather like a worm. The turtle wiggles its "worm" and inquisitive fish, thinking they have found an easy meal, swim straight into its mouth.

A group of fish — the anglerfish — use a similar hunting tactic. Anglerfish are lump-shaped fish very well camouflaged to look like stones, seaweed, or some other part of the surroundings. Just above the mouth is a wiggly worm-like lure. An anglerfish has a huge mouth, and before its prey reaches the lure, it opens its mouth and sucks its dinner in.

▼ Young copperhead snakes have bright yellow tips to their tails. By wiggling these, they can attract the attention of passing frogs and lure them to their death.

▲ The alligator snapping turtle's worm-like lure attracts fish right into its mouth.

More about ⟫ Lures p 29 Snake disguises p 30, 31, 49, 50
Spider camouflage p 22, 39, 51

Heads or tails?

Camouflaged shapes can be so confusing that it is difficult to tell an animal's head from its tail. Some animals have large distinctive eyespots that look just like real eyes from a distance. Others have special markings that blend so well with the environment that it is hard to tell where the animal begins and ends.

◄ Eyespots help to distract a predator's attention from the more vulnerable head.

Two heads are better than one

An animal's head is the most delicate part of its body. If its head is attacked, it may be blinded, or it may lose its feelers or another important sense. By having false eyespots in a less important part of the body, it distracts the predator's attention from its head. Many butterflies have eyespots near the edges of their wings, and it is not uncommon for butterflies to be found with a chunk bitten out of their wings around the eyespot — evidence of the success of this camouflage.

The second "head" on this hairstreak butterfly is made from special markings and streamers on its wing tips. While at rest, the butterfly waves the streamers to look like antennae (feelers). The stripes on its wings all lead to the false head, improving the camouflage. When it lands on a leaf, it turns around so that its false head points in the direction from which it came. If it is disturbed, it quickly flies off in the opposite direction.

Butterflies and fish often have their own eyes well masked by dark stripes, while they have false eyes at the other end of their bodies. So, it is difficult to work out where their head is. The four-eye butterflyfish, which has a large eyespot near its tail, adds to the effect by slowly swimming backwards, but if it is disturbed it will shoot off in the opposite direction.

◄ This butterflyfish has a stripe to conceal its real eye, and a false eye near its tail.

Sitting pretty

If an animal's background is strongly patterned, it may need to take up a special position to match. Some moths that have bark-like markings take up just the right position on a tree trunk so that the direction of their markings will match the pattern on the bark. Scientists have discovered that the moths work out how to sit by feeling the pattern of ridges on the bark.

Swallowtail butterfly pupae, which have a leaf-like shape, are placed exactly halfway between two leaves on a stem. In this position they look like another leaf.

The bittern, a large bird that lives in reed beds, has a brown and white striped breast and neck so that it matches the pattern of the reeds around it. When it is alarmed, the bittern "freezes" with its head pointing up so that the stripes on its belly and neck seem to disappear into the sky, just like reeds. It may even sway from side to side as the reeds blow in the wind. If you walk around the bird, it will slowly turn so that it remains facing you. This makes sure that you will always see the bird's camouflaged side.

The nightjar rests with its body lined up to lie along the branch rather than across it, like most other birds, so that its shape blends with that of the branch.

▲ Hawk moth caterpillars, which have vein-like markings on their bodies, sit so that their mock veins make the correct angles with the stem.

▲ A caterpillar with two heads?

▶ The mottled beauty moth takes up a position where its markings match those of the tree trunk.

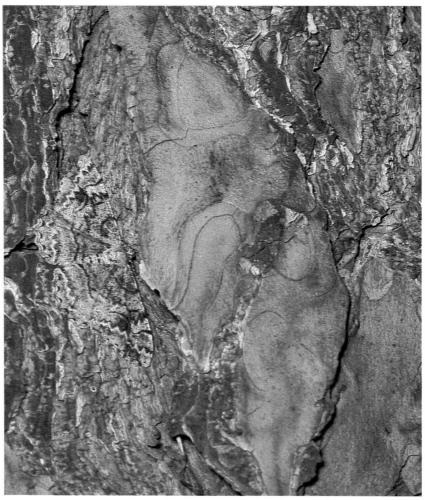

More about 》》 False eyes p 46-49 Choosing the right position p 9, 21-23, 30-32, 40
Hiding eyes p 25, 26

The decorating business

When a birdwatcher wants to camouflage a hide, he will collect branches, sticks, and leaves to cover it. Some animals also use material from their surroundings to camouflage themselves.

Growing gardens

Spider crabs have triangular-shaped bodies and long thin legs. They pick up small pieces of seaweed, sponges, and similar types of materials and fix them to tiny hook-shaped hairs on their bodies. As time goes on, other sea creatures and seaweeds start to grow in this "garden," until the crab looks like a walking piece of seabed.

▲ A spider crab decorates itself with weed and shells for a perfect camouflage.

◄ A hermit crab shares its home with four sea anemones.

For other small creatures that live on the seabed, such gardens grow without any help. Sand and silt settle out of the water and collect in between the ridges on the shells of sea snails, clams, and mussels. Seaweeds and small sea animals soon start to grow in these sediments.

On land, there are the decorator insects — bugs, grasshoppers, and even caterpillars who fix pieces of

Caddis creations

Caddis flies are rather like a cross between a moth and a fly, with papery brown wings and long antennae. Their grub-like larvae live underwater and feed on water weeds. Caddis larvae make their own homes by fixing together stones, shells, or pieces of weed to provide a perfect camouflage. They can cut accurate lengths of leaves and fix them in a neat spiral, or in parallel rows to form a tube. Each type of caddis fly produces a different kind of case. As the larvae grow, they add more material to the front of the case.

If you keep caddis larvae in an aquarium, you can give them different kinds of materials, such as water plants, tiny glass beads or pieces of sticks, and watch how they make their cases.

leaf and debris on to stiff hairs and bristles on their bodies. Some caterpillars that live on lichen-covered tree trunks have a complete coating of lichens over them.

Borrowed houses

Hermit crabs inhabit old mollusk shells. When not feeding, they retire into the shell and close the opening with their large claw. Then they can roll about in the waves like empty shells. Seaweed and many kinds of other sea animals live on these shells. It is common to see such a shell covered with several large sea anemones and the wiggly white tubes of feather worms.

▶ Caterpillars of the bagworm moth make homes of plant fragments, binding them together with silk.

Covered in corpses

A rather gruesome kind of camouflage is used by some insects, which cover themselves with the corpses of their prey. Lacewing larvae suck the juices out of their greenfly (aphid) victims, then stack the remains of the bodies on their backs. Some African bugs collect ant corpses in the same way.

Sponge hats

The sponge crab uses a living sponge instead of a borrowed shell. It cuts off a piece of sponge and wraps it around its back. Then the sponge grows to cover the crab. Sponges often have a rather unpleasant taste, so many animals avoid eating them. This helps the crab to avoid being eaten, too.

More about ⟫⟫ Coats of stones p 38 Looking like seaweed p 7, 9, 23, 26, 41
Underwater camouflage p 7-9, 12-14, 18-21, 23, 26, 28, 29, 32, 41, 45

Animal, vegetable, or mineral?

▲ Not a piece of lichen, but a caterpillar covered in lichen.

Some animal disguises are so clever that it is difficult to tell whether the object you are looking at is animal, vegetable, or mineral. A pile of earth may suddenly start to move, or a tortoise may appear to turn into a stone as it withdraws into its shell. Twigs start to walk, dead leaves suddenly fly away, and pretty flowers reach out and grab passing insects.

In some cases, camouflage is near-perfect. The stonefish's camouflage is so successful that divers have sometimes accidentally stepped on its poisonous spines.

Pebble dash

Coats of stones, soil, and sand are quite common. Dahlia sea anemones coat themselves in bits of shell and stone. With their tentacles drawn in, they look like little rings of stones. Grasshoppers and bugs fix stones between stiff hairs on their backs, and moths stick pieces of bark to their cocoons to camouflage them. Some of the juicy South African desert plants have sticky hairs on their leaves to which dirt and dust sticks. This will help to conceal them from the eyes of thirsty animals.

The eggs of birds that nest on pebbly beaches may be just the size, shape, and color of the stones that surround them, making them almost impossible to detect, even if you know they are there.

▲ Just pebbles on the beach?

Bird droppings that walk

Another way animals have of stopping other animals from eating them is to look like something nobody would want to eat. Small insects and spiders sometimes look like bird droppings. After all, what bird would eat its own droppings? The swallowtail butterfly's caterpillars are a quite shiny brown mottled with white, with little lumps and bumps on them, just like a bird dropping. Some bird-dropping caterpillars also rest with their heads curled round to improve the deceit. The alder moth caterpillar spins fine strands of silk across the leaf around it to make it look like the pale edges of a splash of bird dropping.

Spiders that mimic bird droppings tuck their legs under their bodies, so that they look like fat white blobs. Moths, bugs, and beetles all take up positions that mask their true shape.

Some of the African moth caterpillars are too small to make really convincing bird droppings. Instead, they tend to live close together, so that it looks as if birds have been resting on the tree and their droppings have fallen onto the leaves below.

Stone plants

For desert animals, juicy plants are often the only source of water. By eating the plants, they avoid having to drink. A group of plants found in South African deserts has fat juicy leaves that look just like stones. They barely come above the ground, and have flat round tops colored to match the surrounding stones.

▼ The swallowtail butterfly's caterpillar looks like a bird dropping.

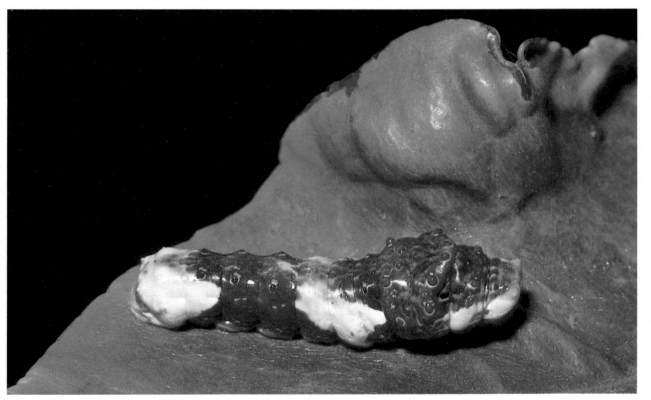

Animals that look like plants

▲ A flower mantis sits perfectly still, waiting for its dinner to fly into its arms.

Animals that like to eat other animals do not usually eat plants, so it can be useful for them to look like a plant. There are all sorts of plant disguises — green leaves, dead leaves, twigs, thorns, flowers, and even seaweed. They are used by several different insects, spiders, frogs, toads, and fish.

Flower mimics

Some of the cleverest of the flower mimics are the praying mantids. Besides matching the color of the flower, they have round flat legs that look like petals, and they sit on a matching flower in such a way that their legs blend with the real petals. The unsuspecting insects that come to feed on the flower's nectar fly right into the waiting arms of the praying mantid.

Moths and bugs sometimes mimic the drooping large-petalled flowers that grow in large clusters in some plants. The wings mimic the petals, and the moth or bug sits in such a position that it appears to be one of the flowers in the cluster. But these creatures are not hunters — they are hiding from their predators.

Not so dead wood

Moths, caterpillars, and stick insects may mimic twigs, with light patches that look like broken ends. Tiny bumps and lumps on stick insects and caterpillars mimic the bark. Sometimes their heads are shiny, so they look like buds. These insects stand at a special angle to look like side twigs, or press themselves flat against the twig. Potoos (nocturnal birds that rest on tree stumps during the day) and frogmouths (owl-like birds from Australia) point their heads skyward to mimic the end of an old stump.

Leaf mimics

All sorts of insects mimic leaves. Besides having brown bodies, they have imitation shadows and markings that look like leaf veins. Moths, butterflies, and katydids (related to grasshoppers), whose own veins run in the wrong direction, have darker vein-like markings which are arranged like leaf veins, with a main vein running down the middle. Pointed wing tips or even antennae may look like leaf stalks.

The mimics even show ready-made decay! Special markings look like the dull decaying brown spots you get on old leaves. The wings of some katydids look as if an animal, perhaps a hungry caterpillar, has taken a bite out of them. One strange leaf insect mimics a leaf that has almost been bitten in two. Its front legs are flattened and leaf-like and they curve forward to cover its head. Other insects draw their legs in close to their bodies or stretch them out behind to avoid detection.

Some frogs and fish also mimic dead leaves. Leaf-mimic frogs live among the dead leaves on the forest floor. Leaf-mimic fish drift near the water surface among the floating leaves.

▶ This butterfly looks like a dead leaf when its wings are closed, like the one at the top of the picture.

▼ A moth mimics a flower.

The leafy seadragon

This extraordinary fish looks just like a piece of seaweed. It is a kind of sea horse, and swims using tiny transparent fins. Other fish look less convincingly like seaweed or seaweed-covered rocks, with fins that look like fronds of weed, or tiny flaps of green or red skin all over their bodies.

More about ⟫ Potoos p 31 Dead-leaf mimics p 6, 7, 11, 24, 30, 32, 33, 37
Plants that look like animals p 42, 43 Stick mimics p 22, 25, 30, 45

Plants that look like animals

Animals are not the only living things that use camouflage. Plants can be great deceivers, too. Plants may look like animals, or they may smell like animals. Their camouflage may help them to use real animals to carry their pollen from one plant to another, or it may lure unsuspecting animals to their deaths.

The sex life of flowers

In order to reproduce, plant flowers produce pollen, a yellow powder that contains the male sex cells of a plant. The eggs of a flowering plant are produced in the ovary, a round chamber situated in the middle of the flower. At the top of each ovary there is a spike called the style. The style has a sticky tip, which is called the stigma.

A plant can only produce seeds if the pollen from one flower lands on the stigma of a different flower. The pollen grows down to the ovary where it fertilizes the eggs. These eggs will then start to develop into seeds.

The go-betweens

Many plants use insects to carry their pollen from one flower to another. Usually they are rewarded with sweet-smelling nectar. But some orchids are much less kind. Their flowers look and smell

rather like female insects. As insects do not have such sharp eyesight as us, they are easily taken in by this deception. The poor males fly in and try to mate with the flower. As they do so, pollen sticks to the hairs on their bodies, and is carried off to the next flower. The insects cannot get anything out of this, they just waste a great deal of energy.

Some orchid flowers look like bees, with furry brown petals. Others mimic flies or wasps and have flowers that look as if they have heads, feelers, and wings. But the flowers do not even need to look very much like insects, as long as they smell right.

▲ A bee is fooled by the bee orchid's disguise.

▼ A fly orchid, which looks and smells like a fly, waits to be pollinated.

A rotten story

Many insects, especially flies, are attracted to rotting meat. Flies lay their eggs in rotting meat, so their maggots will be surrounded by food when they hatch. All sorts of plants look and smell like rotting meat, with reddish brown mottled flowers and a strong, unpleasant smell of decay.

Clusters of fly eggs can often be seen on the flower. The cost to the flies is very high. They waste their eggs by laying them in a place where the maggots will starve.

▼ Flies are attracted to the warm arum flower.

Kidnapped!

Arums are even more cruel. They lure insects deep into the flower by a combination of smell and warmth. Here, chemical reactions in the spadix — the dark column in the center of the arum flower — produce a lot of heat.

Once inside the flower, the insects are trapped by the backward-pointing hairs. They crawl over the ovaries in search of food. After a few days, the stamens burst open, and these trapped insects become covered in pollen. Now the hairs wither, and the insect can escape, to repeat the performance and deposit their pollen on the ovaries of the next arum flower that they visit.

▲ Flies have laid their white eggs in the center of this carrion flower, thinking they have found a juicy piece of meat.

Plants that lay eggs

The brilliant Heliconia butterflies that live in the forests of Central and South America lay their eggs on passion flower vines. When they hatch, the caterpillars feed on the leaves of the vines. But the vines are fighting back. Heliconia butterflies will only lay their eggs on leaves and stems that do not already have eggs on them. This makes sure that their caterpillars will have enough food. The passion vine produces mock eggs, which discourage the butterflies from laying their eggs on the vine.

More about ⟩⟩ Bee mimics p 54, 55 Disguising smells p 51
Plant disguises p 38, 39

Babies in disguise

Remember the story about the ugly duckling that grew up to be a beautiful swan? Well, there was an extremely good reason why the baby swan was ugly — he was safer that way. His brown fluffy coat was far less conspicuous than the brilliant white feathers of his parents.

Most baby animals need a lot of protection from their predators. They often have much better camouflage than their parents.

Spots, speckles, and stripes

Many quite plain animals have babies that are very beautifully patterned. Spots, speckles, and stripes make very good camouflage, and baby lions, pumas, and deer have spotted coats. Baby wild boar (pigs)

▲ Mute swan with cygnets.

▼ Baby wild boars have spotted coats, which blend with the flickering sunlight and shadows on the forest floor.

and tapirs are striped. Even the dismal gray alligator produces young that are speckled and striped to blend with the weeds by the edge of the water.

Birds' eggs are often covered in brown·blotches to disguise them. Gull and tern eggs look just like the other pebbles on the beach where they are laid. The baby birds that hatch are also well camouflaged, especially if their nest is on the ground.

Caterpillars also need to be well camouflaged in order to protect them from the beady eyes of hungry birds. But their butterfly parents can fly away, and they are often very brightly colored. Their vivid colors and patterns often play an important part in courtship displays and rituals.

▲ Young alligators have striped and speckled coats for camouflage among the water weeds.

Guess the parents

Some babies look quite unlike their parents. The see-through camouflage and bizarre shapes of many sea babies are not a bit like the colorful fish, starfish, crabs, shellfish, and prawns that produced them.

Some praying mantids show a remarkable range of camouflage. The babies at first look like ants. They even behave just like ants, darting to and fro, and holding their front legs off the ground to look like the ants' antennae (feelers). When they have grown too big to look like ants, the baby mantids start to mimic scorpions instead. They curl up their abdomens to look like scorpion tails and hold their front legs forward like pincers. The adults mimic dead leaves and twigs.

▲ The transparent larvae of a crab, a sea urchin, and a barnacle float near the surface of the ocean. Their see-through bodies give them near perfect camouflage so that they can escape from their predators.

See-through babies

The young of fish, starfish, sea snails, crabs, shrimps, and many other kinds of sea creatures are very tiny at first. They live in the surface waters of the oceans, where it is very clear and bright.

Here, a transparent (see-through) body is the best type of camouflage. Millions of these microscopic animals float in the oceans, looking like intricately sculptured glass ornaments.

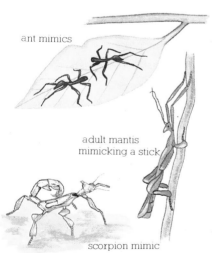
ant mimics

adult mantis mimicking a stick

scorpion mimic

More about 〉〉 Ant mimics p 33 Camouflaged eggs p 38, 56
Transparent animals p 8, 29

Acting big

Many animals try to make themselves look bigger when they are threatened. Have you ever watched a cat that has been cornered by a big dog? The cat arches its back and fluffs up its fur so that it looks much bigger than it really is. Then it shows its teeth and hisses like a snake. Often this is enough to make the dog back away.

Whether the dog really thinks that the cat is a big animal, or even a hissing snake, we shall never know. Usually the dog gets such a nasty surprise that it does not hang around to find out!

▲ The great horned owl chick fluffs up its wing and head feathers so that it looks like an enormous face.

▼ The brightly-colored ruff of the frilled-neck lizard frightens away predators.

Fearsome frills

The frilled-neck lizard that comes from Australia has a collar of skin around its neck that it can spread like a large ruff when threatened. The ruff is decorated with a glowing pattern of black, white, brown, and red, with yellow spots. As if this display were not enough, the frilled lizard will often stand up on its hind legs, and wave its large whip-like tail as if to lash at the enemy. The lizard also hisses, opening its mouth wide to show the bright yellow lining, a color that signals danger to most animals.

All fluffed up

A young owl will put on a fierce display if frightened, fluffing up its outspread wing and head feathers until it looks enormous. With its huge eyes glaring at the intruder, it looks like the face of a much larger animal. It snaps its beak open and shut, sways from side to side, and lunges forward at the enemy.

Hard to swallow

Pufferfish are masters of inflation. Puffers are spiny fish that range from 10 inches to 2 feet long. Their bodies are flattened, and the spines

The inflation game

Some animals can suck in air and pump up their bodies like balloons. Toads and chameleons will blow up their bodies with air and stand on tiptoe. Anolis lizards will blow out a large, brightly colored throat sac to flash warning red and yellow at the enemy. But the masters of inflation are the pufferfish, which can blow themselves up to look like large spiny floating balloons.

point backwards. But when the puffer is alarmed, it rapidly gulps in air or water to blow up its body into a spiny ball. Then it turns upside down and floats at the surface of the water, looking for all the world like some strange prickly tropical fruit.

With all its stiff spines, a fully inflated pufferfish is almost impossible to swallow.

Standing up to the enemy

Four-footed animals like bears and some very large lizards will rear up on their hind legs when threatened, often towering over their attackers. Cobras rear up and flatten out their necks to form a flattened "hood," which makes them look much bigger. Sometimes the hood bears a pattern of two large eyes for an even more fearful effect.

Elephants spread their ears out as they charge towards an animal — or a human — that is annoying them. This makes the angry elephant look even larger than it really is. A charging elephant can be extremely dangerous, so watch out for these expressive ear signals.

◀ This South American false-eyed frog is showing its bottom to an intruder. When it inflates its body, two large eye spots appear on its bottom, so the intruder is faced with what looks like the eyes of a very big animal.

More about ➤➤ Red warning colors p 15, 18, 19, 48-53, 55 Acting big p 48, 49
Surprise colors p 48, 49 False eyes p 34, 48, 49 ➤

Surprise! surprise!

▲ When alarmed, the fire-bellied toad rolls over on its back and puffs up its belly to display its bright warning colors.

Bright colors are used for many different purposes in the animal kingdom. They attract mates, help animals recognize each other, and warn of danger. Reds and yellows in particular are used to threaten and warn. Many animals, ranging from stick insects to elephant seals, use sudden displays of warning colors to frighten off intruders.

Red bellies

A sudden show of bright colors can be enough to frighten off a predator. Some moths, mantids, and stick insects have bright red or orange underwings. When attacked, the moths flash their wings and fly away while the predator is still confused. The mantids rear up and flash their warning colors, at the same time showing other color shapes on their swollen forelegs. Mantids have been known to frighten away monkeys by this threatening display. As each kind of mantid has a different display, predators do not usually learn to recognize the bluff.

Several toads and frogs have brightly colored bellies. When attacked, they will roll over on their backs and puff themselves up, lying stiff and still in the hope that the attacker will heed the warning and go away.

Big brother is watching

Imagine you are a bird about to eat a large juicy moth, when suddenly a big red face with huge eyes is staring right at you, and the moth is nowhere to be seen. Many dull-looking moths and bugs will suddenly open their wings wide to reveal brilliantly colored underwings that are decorated with a pair of large "eyes," just like the face of a much larger animal.

▼ A frightened silkmoth displays a large pair of eyes.

Crab-eyed gobies, little Australian fish, raise the fins on their backs to show a pair of large eyes. The dark fins on their bellies look rather like a pair of pincers, and the overall effect is of a fierce crab looking straight at you. One South American frog even has large eyespots on its bottom!

Snake charm

Some tropical caterpillars look remarkably like tree snakes. When alarmed, they will hang over the edge of the leaf, and puff up the front part of their bodies to display a huge pair of false eyes on what looks like a wedge-shaped snake-like head. They even hiss like snakes and pretend to strike at their attackers. Birds are not very good judges of size, and this deceit seems to work very well.

Disappearing acts

Butterflies and moths often have patterns that resemble dead leaves on the under surfaces of their wings. When at rest with the wings folded, they are extremely difficult to spot. Some, like the huge emperor butterfly, have bright blue shimmering upper wing surfaces. As they fly, you see first a flash of blue as the wings open, then the butterfly disappears as the wings close. This makes it very hard to tell exactly where the insect is at any one moment.

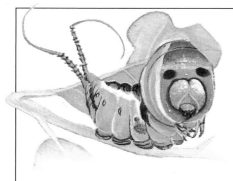

Cross puss

A frightened or angry puss moth caterpillar will draw in its little brown head and puff up its body to display a large red face with two (false) black eyes. Its forked tail arches up over its back and two whips lash at the intruder.

▼ A ringneck snake twists over to display its warning colors.

▼ Once the emperor butterfly closes its wings it almost disappears.

More about 〉〉 Warning colors p 46, 47, 52, 53, 60 Moth surprises p 40, 41, 51, 55 Butterfly camouflage p 9, 34

Covering your tracks

If camouflage alone does not work, the only way to escape from a predator may be to run (or swim) away. But even then, some animals have special ways of disguising their retreat.

Smoke screens

The word "camouflage" comes from an old French word, which means to blow smoke in the face of an enemy. Soldiers use smoke screens to help hide their retreats.

Animals cannot use smoke, but squid, octopuses, and some sea slugs produce clouds of inky liquid as they swim away. Some deep-sea prawns, which live in the darkness of the deep, unlit oceans, produce clouds of luminous particles instead.

▶ A resplendent quetzal, a master ventriloquist, in the jungle of Costa Rica.

Sound tactics

Sounds often give away an animal to its enemies. The quetzals, magnificent birds that live in the jungles of Central and South America, have a rather curious, almost metallic, whistling call that is difficult to place. You just cannot tell the direction from which the sound comes. So the quetzals can call safely to each other in the forest. Many

▼ A sea hare covers its escape with a cloud of ink. By the time the ink has spread out and the predator can see what lies ahead, the sea hare will have vanished.

small birds have extremely high-pitched alarm calls which are similarly misleading.

Other animals use sounds to deceive when they come face to face with an enemy. Many birds that nest in holes in trees will hiss if disturbed. Presumably the predator thinks there is a snake in the hole and does not investigate. Some small caterpillars puff up false eyespots on their bodies and hiss like snakes if threatened. Cats also hiss if they are attacked.

Silent stalkers

Sound can also be a real problem for the hunters, warning their prey that they are coming. The cat family, which includes lions, tigers, and pet cats, are able to draw in their sharp claws so that they do not touch the ground. Cats walk on the soft pads of their toes, and can creep up very quietly on their prey.

Owls, which hunt at night, have very soft feathers that make no noise as their large wings slowly beat up and down. This means that they can glide silently through the forest in search of mice. If their wings made much noise, they would find it difficult to hear the high-pitched squeaks of their frightened quarry.

▲ Lions pull in their claws and walk very quietly on their soft, padded feet.

▲ The fringes on this tawny owl's feathers help to muffle the sound of its movements.

Subtle smells

Many animals identify other animals by their smell. Bees, wasps, and ants are able to recognize members of their own colony by their smell, and may attack outsiders.

Many insects and spiders that live in ant and termite colonies, or prey on the grubs of wasps and bees, produce smells that mimic those of their prey. As insects do not have very sharp sight, having the right sort of smell is often a good enough disguise to allow them to enter nests unchallenged.

Some beetles travel with the great army ant columns in the tropics, feeding on the ants' leftovers. Others feed on the ants' young, or on the waste in their nests.

Radar jamming moths

Bats hunt their prey in the dark by sending out high-pitched sounds and listening to the echoes as the sound waves bounce off solid objects. In this way they can detect the flying moths that will form their supper. But some moths can detect the bat's sound signals, and will produce their own signals to block the bat's system. Just like human troops, they can jam their enemy's radar.

More about ≫ Deep-sea animals p 28, 29 Special smells p 42, 43, 53
Ant mimics p 33 Feathers p 12, 13, 15

Warning colors

▲ Many kinds of animals have bright warning colors.

Some of the brightest colors in nature are used as danger signals. Just as we use red lights, so animals use red, yellow, and orange as warning signals. Usually warning colors come in bold patterns of stripes or blotches — red and black or yellow and black. They are used by animals that are poisonous or have nasty stings or bites. Once a hungry predator has tried to eat one of these, it will not want a second taste, and the bright colors help it to recognize similar animals next time, without taking a bite first.

▼ The bizarre lionfish of tropical seas has poisonous spines.

Stingers and biters

Everyone knows that a yellow-and-black striped insect is likely to be a wasp, and should be avoided. Wasps have nasty stings, but their buzzing and their distinctive bright colors warn us to avoid touching them.

Many hairy caterpillars have poisonous spines, which cause a skin rash if they are touched. They, too, are often gaily colored. The black widow spider, which has a very poisonous bite, has a red cross on her abdomen. She hangs in her web in such a position that the cross is clearly visible.

Under the sea, the lionfish is covered all over in bright red and white stripes. It has very poisonous spines. The deadly poisonous cone shell is a bright orange-yellow, and some venomous sea snakes have vivid yellow and black stripes.

Stinkers

Another way to put off an enemy is to make a nasty smell. Skunks are famous for this. If it is frightened or annoyed, a skunk will rear up on its front legs and point its bottom at the source of the trouble, squirting a bad-smelling liquid at the intruder. Skunks have really striking black-and-white patterns to advertise their unpleasant, smelly defense.

In the family

The caterpillars of some butterflies and moths feed on poisonous plants like ragwort and milkweed. They take in the plants' poisons, and so become poisonous themselves. When they turn into adult butterflies or moths, they continue to be poisonous.

Sometimes all stages of the life cycle of these insects have warning colors. The monarch butterfly is orange and black, but its caterpillars, which feed on poisonous milkweed, have yellow and black stripes.

Butterflies and moths with warning colors often fly very slowly in order to show off their colors better.

They make you sick

Many animals either have a nasty taste or are poisonous, and make any animal that tries to eat them very sick. Arrow poison frogs are so poisonous that the South American Indians used to use them to tip their arrows. They come in a variety of bright colors — orange, yellow, and scarlet — with black spots or stripes.

Some salamanders that have poisonous slime on their bodies also have warning colors. Millipedes are often orange or red. They have both a nasty taste and a very unpleasant smell.

Some poisonous snakes have bright warning stripes, while others, like the fer de

Nasty knees

Ladybirds have their knees to defend them! When disturbed, ladybirds produce a poisonous fluid from their knee joints. Their distinctive red and black colors warn off hungry birds.

lance and the bushmaster, rely on good camouflage to ambush their prey. No one knows for sure why some poisonous animals have warning colors, while others do not.

▼ The bright colors of the arrow poison frog act as a warning.

Copycats

Bright warning colors are very successful in keeping predators away, so it is not surprising that some animals that are not poisonous or dangerous use them, too. They aim to copy or "mimic" animals that are poisonous. The genuinely poisonous animals are "models," and the harmless animals that imitate them are "mimics."

Wasp mimics

The commonest mimics are probably the wasp mimics. Many different insects mimic wasps. Hoverflies live in similar places — on flowers and around rotting fruit. If you take a close look at a hoverfly, you can tell the difference — it keeps its wings spread out when at rest, it has large eyes, and when in

▲ Hoverflies feed on a dandelion.

▼ A lacewing (*below*) mimics a paper wasp (*above*).

the air it hovers around flowers, darting in and out for sips of nectar.

Even moths and beetles can mimic wasps. Wasp-mimic moths have transparent wings. Wasp beetles have yellow and black bodies, and dart to and fro like wasps.

Beastly bees

Some hoverflies mimic bees. They have furry bodies, and make a buzzing sound. Some bee mimics seem to deceive the bees themselves. Bee-mimic hoverflies enter the bumblebee nests and lay their eggs there. The grubs of the hoverfly then feed on dead bees. They also stroke the bee grubs and persuade them to produce droppings for the hoverfly grubs to eat. Some wasp-mimic hoverflies enter wasp nests and lay eggs there for the same purpose.

The numbers game

For mimicry to work well, predators must sample the genuinely poisonous animals more often than the mimics. Only if wasp-like insects usually sting will a predator learn to avoid them. The second rule of the mimicry game is that the models and the mimics must live in the same area, otherwise the predators living in that area will not have a chance to learn what the warning signs mean.

Cheeky salamanders

The dusky salamander from North America is usually a rather dull brownish color, but in certain areas many dusky salamanders have bright red cheek patches. These are areas in which the red-cheeked salamander also lives. As the red-cheeked salamander tastes extremely unpleasant, other animals avoid it, and so the dusky salamanders will benefit from mimicking it. But, in places where the red-cheeked salamander is not found, the dusky salamanders fare better with brown cheeks, which provide better camouflage.

Color codes

In parts of North America, harmless kingsnakes mimic poisonous coral snakes that live nearby. Both kinds of snakes have red, yellow, and black stripes. You can tell which is the coral snake and which is the harmless snake by the order of their stripes.

▼ "Red and yella', kill a fella'," "Red and black, friend of Jack." Can you tell which snake is which in these pictures?

Moth mischief

Some wasp-mimic moths look quite ordinary, with dull brown wings. But, if they are threatened, they will draw back their wings and curl up their black-and-yellow striped abdomens, just like a wasp about to sting.

More about ≫   Warning colors p 46-48, 52, 53 Threat displays p 18, 19, 46-50
Snake disguises p 30, 31, 46, 49

Multiple choice

Does it work?

Many experiments have been done to test whether mimicry works. In most cases, it does. Young birds that are fed nasty tasting butterflies with very bright warning colors will refuse such butterflies in future, even if they are offered harmless mimics. Similarly, after tasting a poisonous salamander, a snake will then refuse to eat any further salamanders with a similar type of coloring, even if it is half-starved.

Changing camouflage

Camouflage also works. In Britain there is a very well camouflaged moth — the peppered moth. By day it rests on tree trunks, and has mottled wings to blend with the lichens on the trunks.

▲ The light peppered moth is much better camouflaged than the dark one on a lichen-covered tree.

Early this century, when the factories produced a lot of dirty smoke, the pollution killed off the lichens, and the soot blackened tree trunks. Now the peppered moths could easily be seen by hungry birds. But among the moth population were a few dark moths. These were now better camouflaged than the pale moths. More of the dark moths survived and, since their offspring inherited the dark color, the population eventually came to contain mostly dark moths.

Now that most of the air pollution has been cleaned up, the trees have lichens again, and the pale moths have increased once more.

Clever cuckoos

We all know that cuckoos lay their eggs in other birds' nests, and leave them to rear their young. Even though many kinds of birds may be used as foster parents, each female cuckoo usually lays her eggs in nests of one particular kind of bird. Cuckoo eggs often match closely the pattern of the foster parents' eggs. If they did not, the foster parents might throw them out. The patterns on the cuckoo's eggs are inherited, but how she knows which nest to lay them in is still a mystery.

◀ The larger cuckoo egg mimics the speckled pattern on the reed warbler's eggs.

A cautionary tale

Not all dull colors are used for camouflage, and not all bright colors are used as a warning, as the following tales will show.

Color problems

Bright colors are used for many purposes in animals and plants. They are used to attract mates, to produce colorful courtship displays, to threaten intruders, and to recognize other animals of the same kind. The bright orange throat sacs that some male lizards use to attract a mate are also used to warn off other male lizards.

Many animals do not have color vision. Do warning colors work for them, or do they recognize the bold patterns of blotches and stripes that often go with warning colors?

Look — no nose!

Why does the polar bear have a white coat? It does not need camouflage as it has no enemies other than humans. Scientists have suggested that a white coat can reduce heat loss, which may help in a cold climate. White coats also save energy — making color pigments uses up energy. But if this is the reason, then why, when it is stalking a sunbathing seal, does a polar bear cover its black nose with its paw?

Some plants produce bright red berries. The color attracts birds to eat them. The pips pass through the birds' bodies and are passed out again. This spreads the plants' seeds to new places. But how do birds know that red berries are for eating, but red animals are to be avoided?

You can see how easy it is to jump to conclusions about colors! We still do not know the answers to these and many more questions about animal disguises.

More about ⟫ Moth camouflage p 6, 9, 21, 24, 25, 35, 40, 41 Egg disguises p 38, 43
Warning colors p 46-49, 54, 55

Bibliography

Danger Colours, OXFORD SCIENTIFIC FILMS, Ed. J. Coldrey and K. Goldie-Morrison, Andre Deutsch, 1986.

Hide and Seek, OXFORD SCIENTIFIC FILMS, Ed. J. Coldrey and K. Goldie-Morrison, Andre Deutsch, 1986.

Survival in the Animal World, F. GEISER AND H. DOSSENBACH, Orbis, 1985.

Camouflage and Mimicry, D. OWEN, Oxford University Press, 1980.

Glossary

abdomen: the hind part of an animal's body containing most of the gut and other internal organs.

algae: simple plant-like growths with no obvious leaves or stems. Algae include seaweeds and millions of microscopic creatures that float near the surface of lakes and oceans.

antennae: the pairs of feelers found on the heads of insects. Antennae are used for touch, taste and smell.

camouflage: a form of disguise that helps an animal to blend with its background so that it is not noticed by other animals.

cocoon: a fluffy ball of silk that moth caterpillars spin around themselves when they are ready to turn into moths.

countershading: a form of camouflage where the animal is colored dark on top and lighter underneath to counteract the effect of natural shadow.

crustaceans: hard-shelled animals with jointed legs and long antennae. The body is divided into three parts, which may be divided into further sections. Crustaceans include shrimps, prawns, crabs, lobsters, and barnacles.

disruptive coloration: coloration that appears to break up an animal's shape and outline.

invertebrates: animals without backbones.

iridescent: describes a surface that shows the colors of the rainbow. The colors appear to change as you look at it from a different angle.

larva (pl. larvae): a young animal that looks quite different from its parents. For example, tadpoles are the larvae of frogs.

lichen: a small, plant-like growth found on trees and rocks. A lichen is a mixture of an alga and a fungus.

mammal: a warm-blooded backboned animal whose body is covered in fur. Female mammals give birth to live young and feed them on milk.

mantis (pl. mantids): a large insect with long forelegs which are used to capture its prey. When not in use, the forelegs are folded rather like hands in prayer, and some mantids are called "praying" mantids.

mantle: the fold of tissue that covers the soft body of a mollusk. The mantle may produce a substance that hardens into a shell on the outside of the mollusk's body.

microscopic: describes something so small that you need to use a microscope to see it.

mimic: an animal or plant that copies, or appears to copy, the appearance, movements, sound or smell of another kind of animal or plant.

mimicry: copying the appearance, movements, sound or smell of another kind of animal or plant.

mollusk: a member of a large group of animals, without a backbone, with a soft body covered by a fold of tissue called a mantle, and a muscular "foot." Many mollusks are protected by a hard shell.

molting: the process of shedding an outer covering of skin, shell, scales, fur or feathers. Some animals molt their skins or shells to allow their bodies to grow. Others shed their fur or feathers to change their color in different seasons, or to replace worn out fur and feathers.

pigment: a chemical produced in the body of an animal or plant that reflects light of a particular color.

plumage: the feathers of a bird.

pollinate: to transfer pollen grains from the male parts of a flower to the female parts.

possum: a small American pouched mammal that lives in trees.

predator: an animal that hunts and eats other animals.

prey: an animal that is hunted and eaten by another animal.

pupa (pl. pupae): a stage in the life cycle of an insect during which it changes from a caterpillar into an adult insect.

refraction: the bending of light rays as they travel from one medium to another, for example from air to water.

reptile: a member of a large group of cold-blooded animals with backbones and a dry scaly skin. Most reptiles live on land and lay eggs covered with a tough, leathery shell.

sea cucumber: a worm-like animal found in the sea, with a mouth surrounded by tentacles at one end.

tapir: a large South American hoofed mammal with a flexible snout.

Index

Acknowledgments

ARTISTS:

David Anstey; Steve Lings/Linden Artists; Mick Loates/Linden Artists; Alan Male/Linden Artists; Maurice Pledger/Linden Artist; Michelle Ross/Linden Artists; Helen Townson; David Webb/Linden Artists; BLA Publishing Limited

PHOTOGRAPHIC CREDITS:

t = top; b = bottom; c = centre; l = left; r = right.

COVER: Michael Fogden/OSF. 6 Eric Chrichton/Bruce Coleman Ltd. 7t E.A. Janes/NHPA. 7b P. Davey/Frank Lane. 8t James Carmichael Jr./NHPA. 8b Stephen Dalton/NHPA. 9t Peter David/Frank Lane. 9b Dieter and Mary Page/Survival Anglia. 10l Hans Reinhard/Bruce Coltman Ltd. 10r Alfred Pasieka/Bruce Coleman Ltd. 11t Stephen Dalton/NHPA. 11b Robert A. Tyrrell/OSF. 12 Frieder Sauer/Bruce Coleman Ltd. 13t Mike Salisbury/Seaphot. 13b John Lythgoe/Seaphot. 15tl, tr and b Trevor Hill. 17 BLA Publishing Ltd. 18 Frank W. Lane/Frank Lane. 19t Otto Rogge/NHPA. 19b Zig Leszczynski/Animals Animals/OSF. 20 Animals Unlimited. 21t Dick Clarke/Seaphot. 21b L. West/Frank Lane. 22 David Maitland/Seaphot. 23 Tom and Pam Gardner/Frank Lane. 24t Stephen Dalton/NHPA. 24b Peter Johnson/NHPA. Jonathon Scott/Seaphot. 26t Melvin Grey/NHPA. 26b Franz J. Camenzind/Seaphot. 27t Jeff Goodman/NHPA. 27b Kenneth Lucas/Seaphot. 28 W. Rohdich/Frank Lane. 29 L. Campbell/NHPA. 30t Ron Austing/Frank Lane. 30b Michael Fogden/OSF. 31t Michael Fogden/OSF. 31b R. Teede/G.S.F. Picture Library. 32 Melvin Grey/NHPA. 34 Francisco Futil/Bruce Coleman Ltd. 35 Rod Williams/Bruce Coleman Ltd. 36 Michael Fogden/Bruce Coleman Ltd. 37 Kim Taylor/Bruce Coleman Ltd. 39 Bruce Davidson/Survival Anglia. 40 G.I. Bernard/NHPA. 42t Alex Kerstitch/Seaphot. 42b Peter Scoones/Seaphot. 44t Leo Collier/Seaphot. 44b Peter Scoones/Seaphot. 45t Frank Lane. 45b Stephen Dalton/NHPA. 46 Ken Lucas/Seaphot. 48 Peter Ward/Bruce Coleman Ltd. 49 Frank W. Lane/Frank Lane. 50t Frank Lane. 50b Walter Deas/Seaphot. 51t Michael Fogden/OSF. 51b Kathie Atkinson/OSF.